If I Could

Written by Judy Nayer ▪ Illustrated by Marsha Winborn

MODERN CURRICULUM PRESS

PROJECT DIRECTOR: **Judith E. Nayer**
ART DIRECTOR: **Lisa Lopez**

Published by Modern Curriculum Press

Modern Curriculum Press, Inc.
A division of Simon & Schuster
13900 Prospect Road, Cleveland, Ohio 44136

This edition is published simultaneously in Canada by
Globe/Modern Curriculum Press, Toronto.

ISBN 0-8136-1085-0 (STY PK) ISBN 0-8136-1082-6 (BK)

10 9 8 95

If I could be whatever I'd like. . .

. . .I'd be a **FIREFIGHTER**
and climb ladders to save lives.

If I could be whatever I'd like...

. . . I'd be a **LIBRARIAN**
and help kids find books they'd like.

If I could be whatever I'd like...

. . . I'd be a **TOUR GUIDE** and show visitors the sights.

If I could be whatever I'd like. . .

. . .I'd be a **PILOT**
and give rides high in the sky.

If I could be whatever I'd like...

. . .I'd be a **SCIENTIST**
and find ways to save wildlife.

If I could be whatever I'd like . . .

. . . I'd be an UMPIRE
and use signs to show who's right.

If I could be whatever I'd like . . .

. . . for now I'd like to be

JUST ME!